Old Time
Recipes & Notes

*From the farm
and ranch kitchens of the past*

By:
Willie Bob

iUniverse, Inc.
New York   Bloomington

Old Time Recipes and Notes
From the farm and ranch kitchens of the past

Copyright © 2009 by Willie Bob

iUniverse books may be ordered through booksellers or by contacting:

iUniverse
1663 Liberty Drive
Bloomington, IN 47403
www.iuniverse.com
1-800-Authors (1-800-288-4677)

Because of the dynamic nature of the Internet, any Web addresses or links contained in this book may have changed since publication and may no longer be valid.

The views expressed in this work are solely those of the author and do not necessarily reflect the views of the publisher, and the publisher hereby disclaims any responsibility for them.

ISBN: 978-1-4401-3081-6 (pbk)
ISBN: 978-1-4401-3082-3 (ebk)

Printed in the United States of America

Introduction

These are some of the old recipes, used by camp cooks, bunkhouse chefs and farm and ranch kitchens that we have enjoyed so much.

It has been a pleasure to put these together for the enjoyment of those who remember the excellent taste, but not the ingredients.

So enjoy, some tastes from our rich historical past. They did.

Acknowledgements

I'd like to thank my mother, wife, grandmother, mother-in-law and
wife's grandmother and great-grandmother and numerous ranch friends
and hunting camp buddies, whom over the years have enable me to
collect these old hand written recipes of the farm and ranch kitchens of
our past.

Table of Contents

Appetizers

HOT BROCCOLI DIP

3 celery stalkschopped	1 pkg chopped broccoli
1/2 onion,chopped	1 can cream of mushroom soup
1 can mushrooms, drained (4oz)	1 roll garlic cheese(6oz)

Saute celery, onion and mushrooms in small amount of butter. Cook broccoli and drain well. Add soup, melt cheese and combine all ingredients.

CHEESE BALL

2 (8oz) pkg cream cheese	1 tsp Lemon juice
2 cups shredded sharp cheese	1/4 tsp garlic salt
1 tbsp chopped green peppers	dash of salt
1 tbsp chopped pimento	dash cayenne pepper
1 tbsp chopped onion	cup chopped nuts

Combine soften cream cheese and chedder cheese, mixing until well blended, add pimento, green pepper, onion, worcesterhire sauce, lemon juice, and seasoning. Mix well and chill, shape into balls, and roll in chopped pecans. Makes two balls.

CHEESE FONDUE

1 1/4 cup bread crumbs	1/8 tsp mustard
1 cup milk	1/2 lb grated cheese
1/2 tsp salt	3 eggs

Separate eggs. Beat yolks slightly and add bread crumbs, milk, salt, mustard and grated cheese. Last fold in the egg whites, beaten stiff, turn into greased baking dish and bake at 350 degrees for 50 minutes or until a silver knife inserted into the center, comes out clean

Bacon With Bannas

6 bananas	1 tbsp lemon juice
4 tbsp butter	12 bacon slices

Peel the bananas and brush with lemon juice and 3 tbsp of oil. Saute in the rest of the butter in a frying pan until golden brown on all sides and tender. Remove to a platter and in the same frying pan cook the bacon until crisp. Arrange the bacon around the bananas and serve.

Cocktail Sausages

Cocktail sausages (1 Can)	3 tbsp sherry
2 tbsp brown sugar	2 tsp mustard

Use small cocktail sausages. Pour juice of the can into skillet add sugar (brown) and mustard. Brown sausages in the sauce. Add sherry and ignite on tooth picks.

Hot Cheese Balls

1 package snappy cheese	3 tbsp sherry
1/2 cup flour	2 tsp mustard

Let butter and cheese soften together. Add flour, blend well. chill and when ready roll small amounts of dough into small balls. Place on an ungreased cookie sheet in small balls, bake in hot oven for 6 to 8 minutes. Serve hot!!

Devilled Eggs

6 hard-boiled eggs	2 tbsp chopped parsle y
2 tbsp maynonnaise	dash cayenne pepper
2 tbsp sour cream	2 tbsp ground green stuffed olives
dash salt	

Boil eggs until hard, peel and cut length wise. Scoop out the yolks and mash up with all seasonings. Put the filling back into the white egg shells.

MUSHROOMS IN OIL

1 lb mushrooms (small)	1 tbsp fresh onion juice
3 buds garlic	1 tbsp lemon juice
salt and pepper	chopped parsley

Mash the garlic in the oil in iron skillet. Add mushrooms, saute until tender add salt and pepper. Add onion and lemon juice. Sprinkle with chopped parsley and serve.

SAUSAGE BALLS

1 lb sausage-mild	10 oz shredded cheese
3 cups bisquick	

Mix and roll together in balls. Freeze before or after baking. Bake at 400 degree oven until lightly brown

PEPPER RELISH

12 red peppers	3 or 4 hot peppers
12 green peppers	4 large onions
2 pts vinegar	3 tbsp salt
2 cups sugar	

Grind up peppers and onions, drain well add: vinegar, salt and sugar. Cook all ingredients 30 minutes until syrupy. Put in sterilized jars and seal.

SHRIMP DIP

1 lb boiled shrimp chopped	2 tsp vinegar
1/4 tsp celery salt	1 cup miracle whip salad dressing
1 pkg dry green onion dip mix	1-8 oz pkg cream cheese

Mix cheese with ingredients, sprinkle top with paprika and parsley flakes.

CHICKEN NUGGETS

4 chicken breasts-whole   1/2 cup melted butter
1/2 tsp salt   1 tsp basil leaves
1/2 cup dry bread crumbs   1 tsp thyme leaves
1/2 cup shredded parmesan cheese

Bone chicken breasts, remove bone. Cut breast into 1 1/2" squares. Mix bread crumbs, cheese, salt,thyme and basil. Dip nuggets in melted butter and in crumb mixture. Place on foil covered baking sheet. Bake in 400 degree oven until golden brown, serve with toothpicks

GUACAMOLE
(cow-camp receipe)

1 can asparagus   garlic salt
2 tsp onion flakes   tabasco
2 tsp worcestershire sauce lemon juice

Mix to taste.

CHILE CON QUESO

4 thick pcs bacon   1 can tomatoes
1 1/2 lbs shredded cheese   2 chopped onions
4 chopped hot peppers   6 garlic pods mashed

Mix ingredients with melted cheese.

Soups

POLISH SOUP

1 lb polish sausage	salt, pepper
6 eggs, hard boiled	4 cups water
2 beef bullion cubes	

Boil polish sausage for about 20 minutes until cooked good. Boil 6 eggs, peel and slice lengtwise. Have 6 cup of water and bring to a boil now add 2 beef bullion cubes until melted. Add salt, pepper to your taste now cut sausages into half-inch pieces, put into already boiled liquid mixture. Add hard boiled eggs. now boil for about 15 minutes, until beef bullion flavors the sausages and eggs.

BEAN SOUP

1/2 pkg onion soup mix	4 carrots
1 can tomatoes	2 bay leaves
2 celery sticks-cut	2 potatoes-cubed

Cover ham bone and 2 cups beans with water. Add salt to taste, 1 tsp pepper and 1 tsp paprika. Cook slow for about 1 hour, then add the ingredients. Cook about 3 hours slowly.

VEGETABLE SOUP

2 cups beef broth	1 tsp salt
1 qt fresh peeled tomatoes	2 qts water
1/2 jalapeno pepper chopped	1 tsp black pepper
1 cup sliced okra	3/4 cup whole corn
2 long green peppers chopped	3 med potatoes diced
1/2 cup butter beans	3/4 cup diced celery
2 tbsp worcestershire sauce	2 carrots chopped
1 large onions chopped	1 tsp garlic powder

Mix together and cook slowly until all are tender.

MEXICAN BEAN SOUP

2 cups beans	salt and pepper
2 minced onions	2 qts water
2 buds garlic	1/2 cup tomato sauce
4 tbsp olive oil	1/2 tsp chili powder
2 strips bacon	1 tsp oregano

Soak beans 4-6 hours, drain and cover with 2 qts warm water. Mince onions and garlic and fry with olive oil for 2 to 3 minutes(not browned) add to the soup, with bacon minced and browned, add salt and pepper. Cover and cook for approx. 2 hrs slow. Fifteen minutes before done, mix tomato sauce, chili powder and oregano, add to soup.

CORN CHOWDER

4 strips bacon	4 ears of corn	
4 potatoes	1 tsp sugar	
3 big onions	paprika	
4 cups milk	salt and pepper	

Dice bacon and fry until crisp, remove the cracklings. Dice the pealed potatoes and slice the onions thin, add to the bacon grease, fry until tender not brown. salt and pepper and add the scaled milk. Boil the corn 2-3 minutes, scrape from the cob. Add to the milk and vegetables. Add seasonings, let it set for 1 hour. when ready to serve boil it and add cracklings.

PEA PUREE WITH CHICKEN BROTH

1 cup peas, pureed	1/4 cup cream
2 cups broth	1/4 stick of butter

Bring to boil-simmer 3 minutes. Season to taste.

POTATO PUREE WITH BROTH AND MILK

1 cup mashed potatoes	1 cup chicken broth
1 grated onion	1/4 stick of butter

Bring to boil-simmer 3 minutes. Season to taste.

Oyster Soup

3 cups chicken consomme
18 oysters and their liquor

salt and pepper
1 cup dry white wine

Heat the consomme when hot add the wine. When it almost boils add oysters and their liquor, season and serve.

Tortilla Soup

2 lbs hamburger
1 can rotel with green chilies
1 large onion
1 jalapeno pepper
1 can whole tomatoes
2 tsp chili powder
2 tsp worcestershire sauce
pepper

2 gloves garlic
1 can chicken broth
1 can beef broth
1 can tomato soup
1 1/2 cup water
1 tsp cumin
1 tsp salt
3 drops tabasco

Saute and drain first four ingredients,add other indredients and simmer for 50 minutes. 10 minutes before serving add corn tortillas, cut into 1" squares

Potato Soup

1/4 lb cubed salt pork, browned
5 celery stalks-chopped
2 tsp salt
1 tbsp worcestershire sauce
1/4 cup chopped fresh parsley
1 tsp ground pepper

6 large potatoes-cubed
1 bunch green onions chopped w/ tops
1 stick butter
1 can milk
1 tsp paprika

Cover with water and boil. Don't add milk or butter until done. Then add milk and butter, heat to boiling.

Vegetable Soup

Put 2 lbs soup bone in pot, cover with water, add 1 onion-diced and 1 cup celery-diced. Bring to boil for 15 minuttes, then simmer for 2 hours. Add 1 can tomatoes, diced carrots and turnips and drainedd shredded cabbage, 1 can potato and rice soup, 1 can corn and english peas. Salt and pepper to taste. Simmer for 1 hour. Check water regularly.

CHICKEN AND MUSHROOM SOUP

2 fryers cut-up
2 cans cream of mushroom soup
1 bell pepper-chopped

salt and pepper to taste
2 cans water

cut up fryers, add 2 cans soup, salt and pepper, add chopped bell pepper. add 2 cans water and cover with foil. bake at 350 degrees in oven for 1 hour until done

HAMBURGER SOUP

1 can tomato soup
2 lb ground beef
1 can tomatoes

1 can cream style corn
1 pint water

Brown beef in skillet, drain off fat. Add other ingredients and simmer for 30 minutes, stirring often. Add 2 tbsp mustard, 4 tsp vinegar and 1/4 tsp red pepper, while simmering

Salads

CHRISTMAS SALAD

1 pkg lime gelatin
1 cup boiling water
1 can crushed pineapple
1 cup cottage cheese
1/2 cup celery-diced
maraschino cherries-halved

1 pkg 30z cream cheese
1 tbsp mayonnaise
1 tsp lemon juice
1 can jellied cranberry sauce
1/2 cup chopped nuts
1 tbsp chopped pimiento

Dissolve gelatin in boiling water, chill until syrupy. stir in pineapple, cottage cheese, celery,pimiento and nuts. Pour into cake pans-lined with wax paper, chill until firm. Turn out on wax paper. Combine cream cheese, mayonaise and lemon juices, first top of gelatin. Cut squares of cranberry jelly for base. Trim trees with cherry halves.

JELLO SALAD

1 carton cottage cheese
1 box jell-o
1 carton cool whip

1 can crushed pineapple drained
1 can fruit cocktail

Mix cottage cheese and dry jello. Stir in pineapple and fruit cocktail. Add cool whiip last. Chill.

SLAW

1 head of cabbage
1 jar pimientos, chopped

1 can salted peanuts
salad dressing

Shred cabbage (cold) mix well

Waldof Salad

1 1/2 cup diced tart apples
1 cup diced tender celery
3 tbsp lemon juice
3 tbsp sherry
1 tbsp honey

1/2 cup sliced blk walnuts
1/2 cup sour cream
1/2 cup mayonnaise
salt and pepper

Let apples marinate in lemon juice and sherry, for 15 minutes. Have ingredients cold then mix them together.

Cole Slaw

3 lbs shredded cabbage
2 cups mayonnaise
2 chopped onions
1 chopped green pepper
1 cup vinegar

2 tbsp sugar
1 tbsp salt
1 tsp dill seed
1 tsp dry mustard
1 cup salad oil

Sprinkle 2 tbsp sugar over cabbage and toss. Mix all and simmer 3 minutes then poor over cabbage.

Cherry-Bannana Salad

3 oz pkg blk cherry jell-o
1 can sweet pitted cherries
1 small can crushed pineapple

3 bananas
1/2 pt whipping cream
1/2 cup pecan pieces

Dissolve jell-o in 1 cup hot water, add 1 cup juice drained from cherries. Let congeal till just set. Add the rest.

Egg Salad

12 hard cooked eggs (grated)
1/3 cup chopped green peppers
2 tbsp chopped parsley

1/4 cup diced celery
3 tbsp diced pimientos
3 tbsp minced onions

Combine all and add, 3 oz cream cheese, 1/3 cup mayonnaise, 2 tbsp chili sauce, 1 1/2 tsp salt and a dash of pepper. Mix all. Set over night in refrigerator.

ENGLISH TEA GARDEN SALAD

1 stalk celery,chopped
1 green onion chopped
1/2 green pepper,chopped
1 lg can english peas drained

1 hard cooked egg
1 med carrot,chopped
3/4 cup mayonnaise
1 med tomato chopped

Mix all together and refrigerate for about 1 hour.

CHERRY SALAD

1 can bing or black cherries in heavy syrup
1 pkg cherry jell-o
1 can crushed pineapple

1 cup broken nuts
2 tbsp cooking sherry wine

Measure juice from cherries, pineapple and add wine. This should be about two cups. Bring to boiling point and dissolve jell-o, well. When it begins to thicken add cherries, nuts and pineapple. Pour in one large mold or individual molds.

MACARONI SALAD

8 oz macaroni
1 small green pepper,chopped
1 small onion,chopped
1 small jar pimiento
1/2 cup mayonnaise

1/2 cup sour cream
3 tbsp sugar
1 tsp celery salt
1 tsp dill weed

Cook macaroni in salted water and drain, add pepper, onion,pimientos, celery salt,and dill weed, mix well. Blend mayonnaise, sour cream and sugar together and toss into other mixture.

CREAMY COLESLAW

1 small cabbage,grated
1/2 green pepper,cut up
1/2 tsp salt
dash pepper

1/4 cup sour cream
2 tsp lemon juice
1/2 cup mayonnaise/salad dressing
1/4 tsp dry mustard

Grate cabbage, mix mayonnaise, sour cream, lemon juice, salt, mustard, and pepper. Pour over chopped cabbage and green pepper.

Peach Salad

6 cans peach halves   1 head lettuce
1/4 lb nuts chopped   1/2 lb chopped dates
1 small bottle maraschino cherries chopped

Mix together the nuts,dates and cherries. Add enough juice from the bottle of
cherries to make stiff paste. Form the mixture into balls, and fill the center with
the canned peaches. Serve on lettuce and top with mayonnaise.

Raw Vegetable Salad

1 cup chopped green pepper   mayonnaise
1 cup chopped carrots   savory dressing
1/4 lb american cheese,grated
1 cup chopped gabbage

Mix each chopped vegetable with enough mayonnaise to bind. On a leaf of lettuce place a mound of carrots. Place a mound of cabbage on top of the carrots
and top with a mound of green peppers sprinkled with grated cheese. Serve
with savory dressing.

Fruit Salad

4 apples   2 bananas
4 oranges   1 can coconut
1 can sliced peaches   3 grapefruit
1 can drained pineapple   3 boxes raisins

Cut up apples, oranges and grapefruit. Put in bowl. Then pineapple, cherries,
peaches and sliced bananas. Add coconut and raisins.

Cherry Salad

6 oz box cherry jell-o   8 oz sour cream
1 can crushed pineapple   2 cups boiling water
1 can cherry pie filling   8 oz cream cheese

Mix jell-o to boiling water. Add crushed pineapple and pie filling. Congeal
and mix sour cream and cream cheese. Add to top.

Green Bean Salad

1 can French style green beans	1 can pimiento
1 can winter peas	1 sliced onion
1 cup chopped celery	

Put in dish. Heat 1 cup sugar and 1 cup salad vinegar. Add 1/4 cup cooking oil. Cool and pour. Let marinate 4 hours. Keep in refrigerator.

Carrot Salad

3 oz pkg orange flavored gelatin	2 cups grated carrots
1 1/2 cups boiling water	8 oz crushed pineapple
1/2 cup flaked coconut	1/4 cup chopped pecans

Dissolve gelatin in boiling water, drain pineapple and add juice to gelatin mixture. Chill until consistency of unbeaten egg white. Stir in pineapple carrots, coconut and pecans. Pour into lightly greased 1 qt mold, child until firm.

Hot Chicken Salad

2 cups chicken, cooked/deboned	1 chopped celery stick
1 can cream chicken soup	1 small jar pieiento
1/2 cup nuts	1 cup chopped onion
1/2 cup mayonnaise	

Mix together and top with shredded cheese and crushed crackers. Bake at 350 degrees for 30 minutes or until bubblly.

Potato Salad

3/4 cup mayonnaise	3 eggs
1 can ppimiento chopped	6 potatoes
1/2 cup chopped onion	3/4 cup pickle relish
1 cup celery chopped	1 tsp salt
garlic powder to taste	

Cook potatoes. Cut into small pieces. Cut up hardboiled eggs and add with pickle relish and pimiento. stir, add onion, celery, salt and stir well. Add mayonnaise and mix

5 Cup Salad

1 cup sour cream
1 cup crushed pineapple
1 cup minature marshmellows

1 cup shredded coconut
1 cup mandarin oranges coconut

Mix and chill.

Cottage Cheese Salad

1 small carton cottage cheese
1 small can crushed pineapple
1 small carton cool whip

1 sm pkg cherry jell-o

Drain pineapple – mix well – and chill.

Miscellaneous Stews

BRUNSWICK STEW

3 cups cooked chicken
1 1/2 lbs ground beef
1/2 lb lean sausage
1 large onion
1 large bottle catsup
3 potatoes,creamed
2 cans tomatoes,mashed

2 cans yellow cream corn
1 can english peas
1 tbsp vinegar
1 tbsp dry mustard
1/4 tbsp red pepper
1 tbsp hot sauce

Cook together beef,pork sausage meat and onion in 1 cup chicken broth and add enough water to cover meat. Cook slowly 1 hour, salt to taste each ingredient. Add catsup,tomatoes and potatoes. Cook another 1 hour. Add english peas, corn,chicken, pepper,hot sauce,mustard,vinegar and cook slowly and stir often. Cook until stew is thick.

IRISH STEW

2 lbs mutton
6 potatoes
6 carrots
6 onions
1 small yellow turnip, cubed
3 sprigs parsley

2 tsp salt
1/4 tsp pepper
2 tsp sugar
3 tsp dark caramel
flour

Cut mutton in inch cubes, add cold water to cover, measuring it, and bring to a boil. Add potatoes, cut in eighths, carrots cut in strips, small whole onions, the turnip cubed, parsley,salt,pepper,sugar and dark caramel. Cover closely and simmer slowly for 2 hours or until meat is tender. for each cup of water stir in 1 tbsp of flour mixed Smoothly with an equal quantity of cold water and stir gently until it boils. Then cook slowly for about 10 minutes. If baked in oven add 1/2 hour cooking time.

CLAM CHOWDER

1 pt clams and juice	1 qt scalded milk
4 cups potatoes, sliced	2 tsp salt
3 sliced onions	1/8 tsp pepper
1/4 cup diced salt pork	2 cups boiling water

Strain juice(clam). Salt pork, add onion and cook until light brown, add potatoes, boiling water, salt and pepper. Cook 10 minutes, add clam juice and cook 5 minutes. Add milk just before serving. Top each serving with halves of crackers.

OYSTER STEW

1 pt oysters with juice	1 tsp salt
4 tbsp butter	1/8 tsp pepper
1 qt milk	paprika

Place oysters, juice and butter in saucepan. Simmer gentlly until edges of the oysters curl. Quickly add milk and seasoning, heat and serve.

COWBOY GOULASH

2 1/2 lbs round of beef	1 cup tomatoe puree
1 1/2 cups chopped onions	2/3 cup red wine
3 tbsp butter	2 tbsp sweet paprika
1 cup beef broth	1 tbsp flour
1 cup sour cream	

Cut the meat in inch cubes and scar it with garlic,onions and butter. mix with paprika and cook 3 minutes, then blend in flour. Add tomatoes,salt,pepper,wine and broth. Cover an simmer gently for 1 1/2 hours or until the meat is tender. If needed thicken the sauce with a little flour, then add the sour cream. Serve with freshly boiled shell noodles.

STEW BEEF AND NOODLES

Melt 2 tbsp of butter in frying pan. Add stew beef cut in small pieces, one onion(diced), and salt and pepper to taste. 2 pods of garlic. Let fry until almost done. Pour in bowl and make gravy in frying pan. Put meat and onion in gravy. Simmer for 10 minutes. Pour over cooked noodles.

Beef Curry

2 lb cubed beef	1 apple-pared/.sliced
1/2 cup chopped onion	1 1/4 cup water
1 pod garlic	1 tbsp curry powder
4 tbsp butter	1 tsp salt
1/2 cup water	1/4 cup flour

Cook chopped garlic in butter. Add cubed beef and brown. Add apple slices, 1 1/4 cup water, curry powder and salt. Cover , simmer about 45 minutes, mix 1/4 cup flour and 1/2 cup water, add to beef and cook.

Cowboy Chili

4 lbs chili meat	5 garlic cloves diced
3 tbsp cumin seed	1/4 cup olive oil
1 tps pepper	1 1/2 tbsp salt
1 onion diced	1/4 tsp red pepper
1 cup catsup	2 (150z) cans tomato
2 tsp sugar sauce	2 cups water
1 tbsp paprika	4 tbsp flour

Brown meat,onion and garlic, then add all ingredients except flour and water. Cook at medium heat 1 1/2 hours the last 30 minutes add water and flour, stir(mix).

All Day Stew

2 lb stew meat	1 can english peas
1 can cream of tomato soup	1 cup sliced carrots
4 potatoes,cut in quarters	1 bay leaf
1 can mushroom soup	1 tsp salt

Mix in pot, cover and bake at 275 degrees for 5 hours.

# Vegetables

GREEN BEANS AND MUSHROOMS

2 cans green beans	2 tsp butter
1/2 oz canned mushrooms	1/4 cup water
pinch of salt	

Drain and wash mushrooms. Place green beans in water, add salt and butter. Bring to boil. Then simmer. Cook for 3 minutes, add mushrooms, cook for 2 minutes.

ENGLISH PEAS

4 slices bacon	1 can mushrooms
1 tbsp chopped onions	2 tbsp flour
1 can english peas	1 tbsp sugar

Fry bacon-crisp, drain fat, add onions and sautee, add liquid from peas, thicken with flour. Add sugar and mushrooms. Add peas to sauce and heat. Crumble bacon into mixture.

BAKED EGGPLANT

1 large eggplant	1/2 stick butter
1 large chopped bell pepper	1 celery stalk chopped
2 cups bread stuffing mix	1 large chopped onion
1 cup grated cheddar cheese	salt and pepper to taste

Cook pared, cut up eggplant in salted water til just tender. Drain throughly and mash. Sautee green pepper, celery and onion in butter until transparent. Add drained eggplant, stuffing mix, salt and pepper. Put in buttered casserole and sprinkle with cheese. Bake at 350 degrees for 30 minutes.

CAULIFLOWER TIMBALES

1 medium head cauliflower	1 cup milk
2 beaten eggs	1/2 tsp salt
3 tbsp grated cheese	1/3 tsp pepper

Break the cauliflower into separate flowerets and cook until tender. Nearly fill greased timbale molds or custard cups with the same. Meanwhile combine the beaten eggs, milk,salt,pepper and grated cheese. Pour this custard mix slowly into the molds or cups so that it fills all the interslices. Set the molds in a pan of hot water and bake in a slow oven at 325 degrees for 40 minutes or until a silver knife inserted in the center of the timbale comes out clean. Unmold and serve with tomato sauce.

GOLDEN FRIED ONION RINGS

6 large white onions	1 cup milk
2 beaten eggs	1/2 tsp salt
3 tbsp grated cheese	1/3 tsp pepper

Cut onions into slices 1/4 inch thick, separate into rings. Combine remaining ingredients-dry. Place in brown paper bag. Flour onions, then in put egg mixture, back into flour. Fry, few at a time, in deep hot fat at 375 stirring once with forks to separate rings. When onion rings are golden, drain thoroughly on paper and sprinkle with salt.

SWEET AND SOUR VEGETABLES

1 can green beans-whole-drained	1 can pimiento drained
1 can winter peas-drained	6 stalks celery chopped
1 onion chopped	

Mix ingredients and add sauce.

SAUCE

1/2 cup vinegar	1 tsp paprika
1/2 cup salad oil	3/4 cup sugar
1 tsp salt	

Dissolve sugar. Add other ingredients and pour over vegetable. Let set in refrigerator for at least 3 hours.

SQUASH FRITTERS

2 medium squash-mashed	1/2 cup flour
1 beaten egg	oil
1 tbsp minced onions	2 tbsp milk
1 tsp baking powder	salt and pepper to taste

Mix squash, egg, milk, flour, salt, pepper, onion and baking powder into mashed squash. Drop batter by the spoonfull into hot oil and fry 3 to 5 minutes or until golden brown. Turn fritters once.

PICKLE SLAW

1 cabbage-shredded	1 tsp salt
1 bell pepper	2 cups sugar
1 1/2 tsp celery seed	1 onion
1 tsp mustard seed	1 tsp turmeric
1 pt vinegar	

Boil vinegar mixture. Cool and pour over cabbage. Let set several hours.

CREOLE CORN

1/2 cup chopped celery	2 tbsp flour
1/2 cup chopped onions	2 tbsp sugar
1 small jar pimientos	1 tsp salt
1 tbsp chili powder	2 tbsp butter
1 can of tomato paste	1 can of corn-drained

Saute celery, pimentos, onions and chili powder in butter. Add flour and blend. Add tomato paste, seasoning and corn. Heat completely and serve hot.

CANDIED SWEET POTATOES

4 medium sweet potatoes	1 1/2 cups brown sugar
1 cup karo syrup	1 stick butter
few drops of water	

Peel and boil potatoes until tender. Boil all other ingredients then pour over potatoes after draining them. Bake in oven at 350.

BEER BEANS

2 cups pinto beans
2 lbs ground meat
1 tsp cumin seeds
1 glove garlic
1 onion-chopped pepper

1 tsp chili powder
salt
1 can beer
garlic powder
2 fresh tomatoes(peeled)

Soak beans in water overnight (covered). Drain and add beer. Cook slowly until beer has evaporated. Add 2 qts water and ingredients including some fat from browned meat. Simmer for 3 hours.

BANDITO BEANS

1 can pork & beans
1 tbsp brown sugar
4 slices bacon-chopped

2 tbsp vinegar
2 tbsp catsup
1 onion-chopped

Onion and bacon, fry them drain grease and add beans,sugar,vinegar and catsup. Stir and simmer 30 minutes (must be covered.)

RANCH SQUACH

8 white squash
1 tbsp butter
1 bouillon cube
1 tbsp sour cream
1 beaten egg

1 cup sour cream
1/2 cup bread crumbs
1/2 cup grated cheese
paprika

Wash and cut squash in fourths, cook in little water, salt lightly until tender drain well and mash with fork. Dissolve bouillon cube in sour cream. Add egg and cream. Put in a buttered dish. Top with crumbs, cheese, paprika and mix. Bake at 350 degrees for 30 minutes.

GUMBO

2 slices bacon-chopped
1 onion-chopped
2 tbsp rice

1 qt sliced tomatoes
1 qt okra-sliced
1 bell pepper

Saute onion, rice and bacon until browned. Add tomatoes,okra and pepper. Cook for 1 hour.

Fried Cabbage

1/3 cup butter	2 tbsp sour cream
6 cups shredded cabbage	2 tbsp vinegar
1/2 tsp sugar	pepper
1/4 cup onion-chopped	1 tsp salt

Cook cabbage in butter, when begins to brown, stir and add other ingredients except sour cream, keep stirring. Just before serving add sour cream.

Cow Peas

2 lbs peas	salt and pepper
6 cubes of salt pork	1 tsp sugar
5 green onions	3 tbsp butter

Put butter in pot, add chopped onions and simmer for 2 minutes, add peas and other things and 3 tbsp water. Cover and cook until tender, adding water when needed.

Potato Pancakes

4 potatoes	2 beaten eggs
1 onion	salt and pepper
3 tbsp flour	bacon grease

Grate potatoes and onion, add other things. Fry just like pancakes on hot griddle until brown and crisp.

Camp Spinach

1 1/2 lbs spinach	3 tbsp butter
2 chopped onions	salt and pepper
1 chopped pepper	garlic powder

Put the butter in a pot, add the onion, salt, pepper and saute 2 minutes. Add other seasoning and spinach. Cover and steam until tender, 4 or 5 minutes.

CAMP RICE

1 cup grated cheddar cheese   1 cup rice
1/2 cup chopped onion   2 tbsp butter
1/2 cup chopped mushrooms   pepper and salt
4 beef bouillon cubes   2 cups water

Mix all ingredients other than cheese in iron skillet and boil, stir often, simmer for 5 minutes. Put in a dish and cover. Bake 35 minutes at 375 degrees, put in cheese and stick of butter, cover and bake 10 more minutes.

FRENCH FRIED ONION RINGS

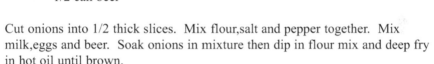

4 large onions   cooking oil
8 cups milk   2 beaten eggs
4 cups flour   salt and pepper
1/2 can beer

Cut onions into 1/2 thick slices. Mix flour,salt and pepper together. Mix milk,eggs and beer. Soak onions in mixture then dip in flour mix and deep fry in hot oil until brown.

SCALLOPED RICE AND MUSHROOMS

2 cups hot,seasoned cooked rice   5 tbsp oil
1 – 4oz can mushrooms   salt and pepper
1 seeded green pepper   1 can tomato soup

Combine the rice,tomato soup,green pepper(chopped fine), can of mushrooms with juice and oil. Arrange in greased casserole and bake at 375 degrees for 30 minutes.

SWEET POTATO SOUFFLE

3 cups cooked mashed sweet potatoes

1/2 cup butter (melted)	3 tbsp flour
1/4 cup orange juice	1 cup sugar
1 tsp cinnamon	1 egg
1 tsp vanilla	1/4 cup milk

Mix all together, pour into casserole dish, and bake 30 to 35 minutes at 350 degrees. Put marshmallows on top and cook 10 to 15 minutes until marshmallows are melted. You can also put 1 cup raisins and 1 cup of nuts into mixture.

CORN SCALLOP

1 can (17 oz) cream corn	1/2 tsp sugar
1/2 cup crushed soda crackers	1/2 tsp salt
1/4 cup chopped bell peppers	paprika
1 tbsp chopped celery	1/4 cup melted butter
6 drops tabasco sauce	1/4 cup shredded carrots
1 tsp chopped onions	2 eggs, slightly beaten
1/2 cup shredded cheese	

Combine corn and all other ingredients except the cheese. Mix well and turn into greased baking dish 8x8x2. Top with cheese and sprinkle with paprika. Bake at 350 degrees for 30 minutes or until mixture is set and top is golden brown.

PINTO BEANS

3 cups of dry pinto beans	1 tsp sugar
1 1/2 tsp salt	water
1 chopped jalapeno pepper	1/2 tsp pepper
14 - 1/2 cubes salt pork(14)	1/2 tsp garlic powder

Pick beans, to make sure no bad ones or rocks. Put in pot, add salt pork, jalapeno pepper and water, 1 inch above beans, add sugar. Let come to a boil, add salt,pepper,garlic powder, turn down to low heat and cook for 3 to 4 hours. Stir regularly and add hot water when needed. Wash before cooking.

BOILED CABBAGE

1 head cabbage	1 tsp salt
10 – 1/2 cubes salt pork	1 tsp sugar
water	

Cut cabbage into large pieces. Cover with hot water 1/4 inch, add salt, sugar and salt pork. Boil, turn to low heat cook until tender and water has cooked down.

TURNIP (ANY) GREENS

mess of greens	2 qts water
10 – 1/2 cubes of salt pork	1/2 tsp salt
1/2 tsp sugar	

Wash leaves carefully, strip leaves from stems. Wash leaves twice more. Put all ingredients in a pot and boil. Them turn down to a low heat for 2 to 3 hours, stirring once in awhile. Add salt just before done.

GARDEN PEAS

pea's	water
salt	sugar
salt pork	

You can snap a few peas young and tender peas, put all in a pot cover with hot water. Add sugar, salt pork and salt. Boil and then cook 2 to 3 hours at low heat until done.

Casseroles

GROUND BEEF CASSEROLE

1 lb ground beef
1 cup cooked macaroni
1 can mushroom soup
salt & pepper to taste

1 cup canned milk
1 onion
1 bell pepper

Chop onion and bell pepper. In a skillet, cook onions, bell pepper and ground beef about 5 minutes. Add milk, soup, cooked macaroni. Stir together all ingredients. Pour in baking dish. Cook at 400 degrees approximately 45 minutes.

PORK-N-BEAN CASSEROLE

2 cans pork-in-beans
3 tbsp ketchup
3 tbsp mustard
2 tsp worcestershire sauce
salt & pepper to taste

1 dash hot sauce
1 dash garlic salt
1/2 lb ground beef
3 tbsp brown sugar

Brown ground beef, add all ingredients together and mix well. Bake at 450 degrees for 25 to 30 minutes.

BAKED BEAN CASSEROLE

3/4 cup grated american cheese   3 onions
1/2 cup fine, fresh bread crumbs 6 bacon slices
3 seeded green peppers   4 tbsp butter
2 cans(#2) pork & beans

Cook the onion and green peppers, chopped fine in oil until they are tender and golden brown in color. Then add the beans and combine thoroughly. Arrange in alternate layers with the cheese in a greased casserole dish, having beans on top. Top with the crumbs mixed with 2 tbsp of oil. Arrange the bacon over the top and bake in a moderate oven at 375 degrees for 30 minutes.

TUNA CASSEROLE

2 cup mashed potatoes	green pepper
small amount of grated onion	2 eggs, beaten
1/2 cup grated cheese	1 small can of tuna

Mix well. Pour in greased baking dish. Cook at 350 degrees until brown serve while hot.

RICE CASSEROLE

1 large can mushrooms	2 cups rice
1 tbsp worcestershire sauce	1 stick butter
1 can beef consomme	

Saute rice in butter. Put in casserole dish. Add beef consomme, worcestershire sauce and well drained mushrooms. Cover and cook at 350 degrees for 1 hour.

SQUASH CASSEROLE

1 lb yellow squash	1 small onion
1 1/2 cups grated cheese	1/4 stick butter
6 ritz crackers	1 egg
1/4 cup milk	salt & pepper

Boil squash and chopped onion until tender. Drain, mash and add cheese,butter,milk,egg,salt and pepper to taste. Crush crackers and add crumbs to mixture. Place in a greased casserole dish and bake at 350 degrees for 25 minutes.

CAMP HASH

1 lb ground beef	2 tsp salt
1/2 cup uncooked regular rice	3 onions slice
1 chopped green pepper	1 can tomatoes
1 tsp chili powder	1/4 tsp black pepper

Preheat oven to 350 degrees. In large skillet, cook and stir meat,onion and pepper until meat is brown and vegetables tender, drain, stir tomatoes, chili powder, rice, pepper and salt, heat.Pour into pan. Cover and bake 1 hour.

CHICKEN CASSEROLE

1 can cream of chicken soup	1 chicken
3/4 cup chicken broth	1 stick butter
1 cup sour cream	45 ritz crackers

Boil chicken in salted water until tender. Remove skin and bones. Put in bottom of dish. Pour 3/4 cup chicken broth over chicken. Mix sour cream and cream of chicken soup and spread over chicken. Crumble ritz crackers and mix with melted butter and sprinkle over top. Bake at 350 degrees for 40 minutes. Light brown on top.

BROCCOLLI-RICE CASSEROLE

1/2 cup chopped celery	1 cup rice
1 can cream of mushroom soup	3 tbsp butter
1/2 cup chopped onion	1 lb broccoli
1/2 lb velveeta	

Cook rice in 2 cups water and 1 tsp salt, bring to boil, lower heat cover and simmer 15 minutes, turn heat up for 10 minutes. Cook broccoli separate(boil). Saute onion and celery in butter. Mix all together, add soups and cheese. Put in casserole dish and heat at 300 degrees for 20 to 30 minutes.

PEPPER AND CORN CASSEROLE

2 beaten eggs	1 chopped onion
3/4 cup of milk	2/3 cup pimiento
2/3 cup green peppers	1/2 cup oil
1 can cream corn	1/2 tsp soda
1 cup corn meal	1 tbsp sugar
3/4 cup grated cheese	1 tsp salt

Mix everything but cheese, bake for 30 minutes at 375 degrees. Put on cheese the last 5 minutes.

Eggplant Casserole

1 eggplant, peeled & diced	2 onions, diced
1 1/2 cup grated cheese	pepper
1 can cream of mushroom soup	1 tsp salt
jar diced pimientos	2 tbsp butter
2 beaten eggs	tabasco
1 cup cracker crumbs	1 tsp soy sauce

Cover eggplant with salted water and boil. Let simmer for 20 minutes. Drain and add all ingredients, mix and bake at 350 degrees for about 30 minutes.

Tuna Casserole

1 1/2 cups cream sauce	8 oz noodles
8 chopped green olives	1 can tuna
1/2 lb sauteed mushrooms	bread crumbs
1 cup grated cheese	

Cook and drain noodles. Mix cheese in hot cream sauce. Alternate layers of all ingredients in baking pan, add cream sauce to each layer. Cover top with crumbs, bake for 15 to 20 minutes at 350 degrees.

Sweet Potato Casserole

2 1/4 lbs sweet potatoes	1/2 cup nuts
3 eggs, beaten slightly	1/2 tsp vanilla
1/2 cup coconut grated	1/4 cup sugar
1/2 cup pineapple juice	6 tbsp butter
marshmallows	

Cook potatoes with little salt,mash potatoes and butter and sugar. Cool slightly, add eggs,vanilla,nuts,coconut and juice. Put in dish, top with marshmallow, bake at 300 degrees untl marshmallow are brown.

Meats

FRIED CHICKEN

1 fryer-cut
3 cups shortening
3/4 cup all purpose flour
1/4 tsp black pepper

1 tsp garlic salt
1/2 tsp paprika
1 1/2 tsp oregano

Combine flour and seasonings; roll the cut up chicken in the flour mixture. Using a heavy deep fry pan, fry chicken in shortening at 350 degrees for 12 to 15 minutes on each side, or until tender and crispy brown.

DAGO STEAK

1 lb round steak
2 eggs well beaten
1/2 cup canned milk
salt & pepper to taste

1 tsp garlic powder
1/2 cup cooking oil
1 cup flour

Cut round steak in 1/2 inch strips. Then put strips of meat in a bowl for 5 minutes with eggs.Let set for 5 minutes, add salt and pepper. After setting for 5 minutes take meat strips out of bowl. Add meat meat strips to another bowl of 1/2 cup canned milk and 1 tsp garlic powder. Let set for 10 minutes to marinate. Take meat strips out of bowl and roll in flour coating on all sides. Have grease about 350 degrees in skillet ready. Drop each meat strip in skillet and turn constantly so it doesn't burn.

HAM A L'TALIENNE

2 lbs sliced ham(1" thick)
1 pt canned tomatoes
1/2 cup water

4 peeled onions
black pepper

Put ham in a covered frying pan. Slice onions over ham, add tomatoes, pepper and water. Cover and bake 1 hour at 400 degrees. Then remove ham, and make a gravy of the tomatoe juice and drippings.

Baked Stuffed Lamb Chops

6 lamb chops(2" thick)	2 tbsp butter
1 tbsp minced onion	1 1/2 tsp flour
1/2 cup chopped mushrooms	3 tbsp chili sauce
1 tbsp water	

Melt butter in sauce pan, add minced onion, chopped mushrooms and chili sauce. Simmer for 5 minutes, then add flour, stir well and add the water last. Simmer 2 minutes longer.Cut a pocket in each chop and fill the cavity with some of the stuffing. Arrange in baking pan and bake at 400 degrees for 30 to 35 minutes or until done.

Steak de Luxe

Rub a steak 1 1/2" thick with a cut clove of garlic, boil. When done put on a hot platter, salt lightly. Mean while prepare the sauce.

1/4 lb butter	1 tsp paprika
1 tbsp catsup	1/2 tsp dry mustard
1 tbsp worcestershire	2 tsp lemon juice

Put the butter in a sauce pan, blend the catsup and worcestershire, then add paprika, mustard and lemon. Place sauce pan over low heat and stir until butter is melted, and sauce is smooth. Don't over heat. When done pour over steak.

Corn Beef Hash

2 cups chopped,cooked or canned corn beef
3 tbsp oil   1 tbsp minced onion
2 cups chopped,cooked potatoes   1/8 tsp pepper

Chop meat and potatoes separately having them fine but not mashed. Heat a frying pan, oil and pan fry onions for 3 minutes. Then add beef, potatotes and pepper. When heated thoroughly allow hash to brown, then fold over like an omlet and transfer to a hot platter. If hash seems to dry, add 1 or 2 tbsp hot milk.

Savory Round Steak

2 lb bottom round steak	1/8 tsp pepper
1 tbsp dark vinegar	1 tbsp mustard
2 tbsp oil	1 tbsp vinegar
2 tbsp flour	1/2 tsp salt
2 cups boiling water	1 tbsp dark caramel

Cut meat into strips 3 inches long and 1 inch wide and sprinkle lightly with some flour. Put oil in frying pan, add meat and brown it on all sides. Remove meat and add oil, the flour,salt,pepper,mustard,vinegar,dark caramel and boiling water.

Roast Beef

1 beef roast, 3 1/2 to 4 lbs	1 soup can of water
1 can cream mushroom soup	1/2 tsp garlic powder
1 pkg mushroom soup mix	1 pkg onion soup mix
salt & pepper to taste	

Place roast in pan, sprinkle well with onion and mushroom soup mixes. Mix can of mushroom soup and water. Pour over roast. Cover pan. Leave enough space for steam to circulate. Bake at 250 degrees for 3 hours.

Baked Pork Chops

6 pork chops	2 eggs
1 pkg onion soup mix	2/3 cup bread crumbs toasted lightly
1/4 cup melted butter	

Beat eggs, then mix soup with bread crumbs together. Dip pork chops in eggs then into soup and crumb mixture. Place chops in baking dish. Add 1/4 cup melted butter over chops. Bake at 350 degrees until brown.

SWISS STEAK

4 lbs lean round steak
1/2 cup tomatoes,pureed
1/3 cup chopped onion
2 tbsp chopped green pepper

1 beef bouillon cube
1 1/2 cups water
1/4 tsp pepper
pinch of salt

Wash and peel tomatoes. Peel and wash onions. Wash pepper. Place steak, prepared vegetables, bouillon cube, salt, pepper and water in small baking dish. Bake at 350 degrees for 45 minutes to 1 hour.

PEPPER STEAK

4 lbs sirloin tip steak/thin sliced
jalapeno peppers
cooking oil
salt

pepper
velveeta cheese
flour

Heat oil, dredge meat with flour. Season with salt and pepper. Fry until desired, remove from skillet to baking dish. Top half of steak with cheese and pepper, cover with rest of steak. Heat in oven until cheese melts. Use pan drippings to make gravy.

RANCH HASH

1 1/2 lb ground meat
1 tsp ground cumin
1 glove garlic minced
1 can tomato sauce
3 sauce cans of water

1 cup rice
1/2 chopped onion
2 tsp salt
1 tsp pepper
2 tsp chili powder

Brown ground meat lightly, add chopped onion and garlic, cook until onions are yellow, drain off grease. Add seasonings and 1 cup rice, stir until rice is lightly browned. Pour in tomato sauce and water. Bring to a boil, reduce heat and simmer for 20 to 25 minutes or until liquid is absorbed.

CAMP BURGER

1 1/2 lb ground meat
1/2 lb ground pork
1 1/2 cup quick rice
3 cups water
pepper to taste

1 1/2 tsp salt
1 can tomatoes
1/4 lb mild cheese
8 slices bacon

Put rice in strainer and rinse, then in sauce pan. Pour in water and salt. Bring to boil, then cook at low heat 10 minutes or until water is gone. Prepare baking dish with vegetable shortening, after mixing meat with salt and pepper to taste, put layer of 1/2 cooked rice in baking dish, thin layer of meat, antoher layer of rice, the remainder of the meat pour can of tomatoes over it, puncture layers to let juice seep in. Sprinkle little salt over tomatoes. Cover, put in preheated oven at 450 degrees for 20 minutes, remove cover then bake uncovered few minutes to get desired texture. Lay bacon over top, sprinkle cheese around bacon. Put in oven for 15 minutes or until cheese is melted and bacon is crisp.

CAMP STEAK

3 lbs round steak
1 can mushroom soup
2 tbsp worcestershire sauce

3/4 cup flour
1 onion
salt & pepper

Pour and season meat, pound each side. Brown meat and onion in oil(hot).
Add mushroom soup, cover and cook low heat 1 hour.

BAKED PORK CHOPS

pork chops
lemon slices

brown sugar
salt & pepper

Put chops in baking pan, put slices of lemon on each and sprinkle brown sugar, salt & pepper chops before putting in pan, bake at 350 until done.

Saloon Burgers

3 lbs hamburger
green peppers-chopped
1 can golden mushroom soup

onion soup mix
garlic powder
jalapeno pepper (chopped)

Mix hamburger, pepper, garlic powder, onion soup and form patties. Cook in iron skillet while still cooking pour mushroom soup mix with 2 cans of water over burgers and simmer for 10 minutes.

Camp House Special

2 cans rotel tomatoes
w/green chilies
1 tsp garlic powder
3 tbsp chili powder
2 1/2 lbs ground meat

1 onion
2 cans beans
corn chips
1 pt half & half
1 lb velveeta cheese

Cook meat and onion until done. Add remaining ingredients except half & half and corn chips. Heat slow until cheese is melted. Before serving add half & half and serve on top of corn chips.

Leg of Lamb

leg of lamb
4 garlic cloves quartered

prepared mustard

Trim fat from lamb, make slits in meat and insert garlic cloves. Cover lamb with mustard. Bake at 325 degrees for 1/2 hour per pound.

Ma Ma's Pork Chops

8 pork chops
1/2 tsp garlic powder
1/2 cup flour
1 can chicken rice soup

2 tbsp oil
1 tbsp salt
1 tsp dry mustard

Shake chops in bag with flour,salt,mustard and garlic powder. Brown in oil in skillet, add soup and simmer slowly until tender.

Wild Game

PHEASANT

canned milk	salt & pepper
self-rising flour	oil
garlic powder	1/2 cup white wine
1 can mushroom soup	1/2 cup minced onions

Soak pheasant in canned milk until well soaked. Season flour with all seasoning except soup and wine. Roll pieces of pheasant in mixture(well coated). Fry like chicken. Place pheasant in baking pan and cover with one can of mushroom soup and 1/2 cup of wine. Bake until tender.

RABBIT STEW

1/3 lb rabbit	2 tsp salt
2 cups diced carrots	6 onions
1 bay leaf	3 potatoes
1/2 cup chopped celery	3 tbsp flour
1 tbsp chopped parsley	

Cut rabbit in pieces for servng. Place in a pot with chopped onions, bay leaf,chopped celery and salt. Cover with cold water and allow to cook slowly until almost tender, about 2 hours. Then add diced carrots and potatoes,paired and cut into quarters. Continue cooking until these vegetables are tender,moisten flour in a little cold water and add to stew. When slightly thickened, add finely chopped parsley.

JERKY

1 cup cornmeal	3 tbsp salt
3/4 inch strips venison	2 tbsp pepper

Cut meat into 3/4 inch thick strips. Roll in salt,pepper and cornmeal mix. Hang in sun on line to dry for several days. Must be dry all way through. Store in cloth sack.

Venison Chili

3 lbs cubed venison	3 tbsp chili powder
5 slices bacon	3 1/2 tbsp flour
1 chopped onion	1 1/2 tsp comino
2 minced garlic	1 1/2 tsp oregano

Fry bacon in small pieces, put in pot, add venison after bacon half fried, then put in onion and garlic. When they are sauteed, and flour, chili powder, comino, orengano, salt and pepper. When flour is mixed, add water at least 3 cups, simmer covered for 4 hours.

Ranch House Quail

4 breast – per person	1/4 cup butter
salt & pepper	1 can consomme
1/2 bay leaf	1/2 cup white wine

Sprinkle quail with salt & pepper, melt butter in skillet and brown, slowly over medium heat. Sprinkle quail with flour. Add other ingredients. Cover and simmer 40 minutes untl tender.

Vension Sausage

67 lbs venison	1 lb coriander
33 lbs pork	2 garlic gloves
6 oz black pepper	14 oz salt

Grind venison and pork mixing dry ingredients – coarslely – then mix well. Sample fry patty to taste. Stuff into beef casings – hang up to dry or smoke. Smoke slowly each until flavor is right. To dry – dry let hang about 30 days

Camp Dove

4 breast – per person	bacon slices
1 bottle italian dressing	medium size jalapenos
salt & pepper to taste	

Salt and pepper each dove, put jalapeno pepper in chest cavity. Wrap with bacon, baste with italian dressing. Grill slowly, baste every few minutes until done.

VENISON POT ROAST

4 lbs venison	1 can carrots
shortening	flour
7 potatoes	5 onions
salt & pepper	

Season with salt and pepper, roll in flour. Brown venison in shortening, drain. Add water to cover meat. Simmer 2 hours or until done. Then add vegetables and cook til done.

BAKED SQUIRREL

4 squirrels,cleaned and dressed	glove of garlic
1/4 cup worcestershire sauce	small bay leaf
2 tbsp onion juice	salt & pepper
2 tbsp chopped parsley	1 can bouillon

Flour squirrel and brown in roasting pan, and all ingredients and bake at 350 degrees for 45 minutes. Reduce temperature and bake slowly for another 45 minutes or until tender.

BRAISED RABBIT

1 frying rabbit	1 can milk
seasoned flour	salt & pepper
2 (2 oz) cans of mushrooms	

Cut the rabbit into serving pieces and dredge with seasoned flour. Brown in small amount of hot fat in a skillet, then place in a roasting pan. Add the milk,mushrooms and salt. Bake at 350 degrees for 1 hour or until rabbit is well done.

Mexican Specialties

Mexican Hamburger Casserole

1 lb ground beef	1 can tomatoes
1 onion chopped	1 tsp salt
1 bell pepper chopped	1 cup maraconi
4 tbsp cream cheese	1 cup buttermilk
2 gloves garlic,minced	2 tbsp chili powder
1 can whole kernel corn	

Saute onion,bell pepper,garlic and ground beef in small amount of oil, untl limp, add other ingredients except cheese. Stir until mixed good. Put in greased baking pan. Sprinkle with shredded cheese. Cover and bake at 350 degrees for 45 minutes or until maraconi is done.

Picante

1 dozen jalapeno peppers	1 gallon tomatoes
3 cups onions chopped	1 cup garlic
chopped	

Remove stems from peppers and discard. Put peppers in blender and chop. Put all ingredients into a big pot, bring to a boil. Turn heat to low and let mixture simmer for 2 1/2 hours then put in canning jars and seal.

Menudo

2 lb tripe	3 pods garlic
1 tsp black pepper	1 tsp salt
2 tbsp chili powder	4 cups hominy

Wash tripe throughly and cut in 1 inch strips. Place in 2 qts of boiling water with salt. Low heat and simmer for 30 minutes. Then pour water out, and start over, when it comes to boil then add hominy and spices and remaining ingredients. Simmer 2 hours, adding 1 to 2 more cups of water to replace lost water.

CARNE GUISADA

1 lb beef(seven steak)	1/2 tsp comino
1 tbsp chili powder	1 lb pork
1 small can tomato sauce	2 tbsp flour
2 tbps shortening	onion,diced
bell pepper diced	garlic glove diced

Cut meat in strips and simmer in shortening. (cover skillet, till meat turns white). Add flour and then brown. Add onion,garlic,pepper,tomatoe sauce,seasoning. Add water to cover. Salt to taste. Then simmer for 1 hour.

NOPALITOS

6 leaves(catus)	3 eggs
1/2 tsp ground red pepper	salt & pepper

Boil leaves after cutting into small pieces for 10 minutes. Then put into frying pan with little butter. Fry 10 mintues, put in 3 eggs and scramble-cook untl eggs are done.

CHILI

16 oz small chopped stew meat	2 diced peppers
1 1/2 cans tomatoes	pinch of salt
1/2 chopped large onion	1 tsp chili powder

Put beef, chopped onions and pepper in pan. Brown, then add chili powder, cook powder into meat for about 3 minutes, stirring. Add tomatoes, let simmer for 15 minutes.

NACHOS

Cut the tortillas into quarters and fry until brown and crisp, drain, put tsp of grated cheese and slice of jalapeno on each piece. Put in hot oven until cheese begins to melt.

ENCHILADA DINNER

2 lbs ground beef
1/2 can rotel tomatoes

1 can beans
1 can stewed tomatoes

Brown meat, salt and pepper to taste. Add tomatoes, 2 green chili peppers diced. Bring to boil then simmer 10 minutes.

GREEN ENCHILDADAS

1/4 cup butter
1 can chicken broth
1 can chopped green chiles
2 pkgs monterrey cheese

1/2 tsp garlic powder
2 tbsp flour
1 pkg 15 tortillas
1 pt sour cream

Melt 1/4 cup butter, add 1/2 tsp garlic powder. When butter melts, add 3 tbsp flour, stir til smooth, add 1 can chicken broth, stir until thickens. Put on low, add 1 pt sour cream and small can chopped green chiles. Fry each tortilla till soft. Roll each with stuffed monterrey cheese, put in dish. Pour sauce over them, sprinkle with grated cheese and bake at 350 degrees for 30 minutes.

VALLEY PICOSO

22 green chiles
2 cans whole tomatoes
4 pods garlic

1 tsp salt
1 lemon

Boil chiles in water, until bright color is loss, peel and put in blender, 4 pods garlic, juice of 1 lemon, tsp salt. Blend until smooth. Add drained tomatoes. Turn on and off quick.

SOPAPILLA

1/2 cup flour
1/2 cup masa harina
1/4 cup buttermilk
1 tsp baking powder

1/2 tsp salt
1/4 cup water
1 tsp sugar
1 tsp shortening

Mix like biscuit dough, roll out 1/8 inch thick. Cut in 3" inch triangles. Put in hot, deep fat until brown.

Hot Tamale Pie

2 lbs ground beef	1 cup chopped onion
1 cup chopped green pepper	4 tsp chili powder
1 can tomato wedges-drained	1 tsp ground cumin
1 can whole kernel corn	1 tbsp chopped pimento
1/2 cup sliced black olives	3 cups cooked cornmeal

Brown ground beef in dutch oven, drain fat. Stir in onion and green peppers. Cook over medium heat 7 minutes, stir in remaining ingredients, except cornmeal and pimiento. Spoon mixture into covered dish. Mix cooked cornmeal an pimiento spread over top of beef mixture. Bake at 350 degrees for 45 minutes.

Cooked Cornmeal

3 cups water	1 1/4 tsp salt
1 cup yellow cornmeal	

In a heavy saucepan, bring water to a boil. Add salt and cornmeal. Cook stirring constantly, until mixture is smooth. Cover and reduce heat to low, cook 20 to 25 minutes, stirring occasionally.

Breads

COWBOY CORNBREAD

3 cups yellow cornbread mix
3 eggs, slightly beaten
1/8 oz can mild jalapenos
seeded and chopped

1 can cream corn
1/2 cup oil
1 onion chopped
1/2 cup bacon pieces

In large bowl, add eggs to cornmeal mix, then oil, corn, onion, cheese, mixing after each addition. Add eggs and spread in generously greased pan. Bake at 350 degrees for 45 minutes.

HOMEMADE BREAD

Start with 1 pkg dry yeast, add 1/2 tsp salt, 2 tsp sugar and 2 cups flour. Mix together with about 1 1/2 cups of warm water. This should be soft dough. Let rise in a warm place about 1 hour. Put in a large bowl and add 12 cups flour, 1/2 cup salad oil and 2 cups all bran and about 4 cups of warm water, approx. Mix together well, let rise. Stir, down twice, let rise 2 to 3 hours. Knead into loaves, let rise 1 hour, bake at 375 degrees for 30 minutes.

BREAD STUFFING

3 qts bread crumbs
2 tbsp chopped celery
2 tbsp chopped parsley
1/2 cup chopped onion

1/3 tsp pepper
3/4 cup butter
6 tsp salt
2 tbsp sage

Combine the crumbs, salt, sage, celery, parsley and pepper. Melt butter in frying pan add onion and simmer gently until tender. Add bread crumbs and stir and heat until crumbs are brown enough for 10 lb bird.

Rice Stuffing

2 cups cooked rice
2/3 cup stewed tomatoes
2 tbsp diced crisp bacon

1/2 tsp salt
1/8 tsp pepper
1 tsp minced onion

Combine ingredients and use as a stuffing for meat or fish.

Hush Puppies

1 cup cornmeal
1/4 tsp baking soda
1 tsp baking powder
1/2 tsp garlic powder

1/4 cup flour
1/2 tsp salt
1 cup buttermilk
1 onion chopped

Stir dry ingredients together(mix well). Add onion and milk(mix well). Drop batter from teaspoon into hot oil. Fry 2 or 3 minutes until browned on both sides. Drain well.

Doughnuts

1 yeast cake
3 cups warm milk
3 tbsp shortening
3/4 cup sugar

2 eggs
1 tsp salt
8 cups flour

Dissolve yeast in milk. In large mixing bowl, mix shortening,sugar and eggs. Blend well, add salt and yeast. Add flour and mix well. Set in a warm place to rise for 2 hours. Roll out and fry in hot oil.

Hot Cakes

1 cup flour
2 tsp baking powder
1 cup buttermilk
2 tbsp shortening

2 eggs
1/2 tsp salt
1/2 tsp baking soda

Mix all dry ingredients and shortening together, add eggs and mix well. Stir only until mixture is wet. Cook on greased hot griddle or skillet

CORN STICKS

1/2 cup sifted flour	2 tbsp sugar
1 cup corn meal	1 cup sour milk
1 egg (well beaten)	1/2 tsp baking soda
2 tbsp shortening	1/2 tsp salt

Sift flour once, measure and add cornmeal, soda,salt and sugar, sift together twice. Combine egg and milk, add to flour mixture stirring only enough to blend. Add shortening turn into hot greased corn stick pans, bake at 425 degrees for 20 to 25 minutes.

SOURDOUGH BISCUITS

2 cups flour (reg.)	2 tbsp sugar
2 tsp baking powder	1/2 tsp salt
1 cup sourdough starter	1/2 cup warm milk

Mix well and turn out onto floured board and knead eight or ten times. The dough should be spongy and slightly sticky. Pinch off a piece of dough, form into biscuit and place on greased pan or(roll out and cut with biscuit cutter). Grease top and set pan in warm place for 20 or 30 minutes. Bake in a 400 degree oven for about 25 minutes or until golden brown. Add to the original starter which was left in the crock, 3/4 cup warm water, 1 1/2 tbsp sugar, 1/2 tsp salt,7/8 cup flour. Set crock in a warm spot to work. After 3 to 4 hours, you can use it in your recipe or store in refrigerator (covered).

PUMKIN BREAD

3 1/2 cups flour	1 cup oil
3 cups sugar	4 eggs
2 tsp soda	2/3 cup water
1 1/2 tsp salt	2 cups pumpkin
1 tsp cinnamon	1 cup chopped nuts
1 tsp nutmeg	

Mix and bake in tube or loaf pan at 350 degrees for 1 hour.

BANANA BREAD

1/2 cup butter	2 eggs
1 cup sugar	1/2 cup nuts
1 cup mashed bananas	2 cup flour
1 tsp vanilla extract	1 tsp salt
1 tsp baking powder	

Cream butter and sugar. Add eggs, then add all other ingredients and bake at 350 degrees for 1 hour.

CRACKLIN BREAD

1 cup self-rising cornmeal	buttermilk
2 cups chopped cracklings	2 eggs
1/2 cup self-rising flour	

Make as cornbread using just enough buttermilk to hold together. Put in greased skillet, bake until brown.

EGG BREAD

2 cups meal(corn)	4 eggs
1/2 tsp baking powder	1 1/2 cup buttermilk

Mix in a large cooking bowl, 2 cups cornmeal, 4 eggs, 1 1/2 cups buttermilk, 1/2 cup melted bacon grease, 1/2 tsp baking powder. Mix all well together. Heat oven to 350 degrees and cook for about 30 to 35 minutes.

QUICK BISCUITS

2 cups self-rising flour	1 cup sour cream

Mix with a spoon, the flour and cream. Makes a soft dough. Generously flour board and roll out. Cut into biscuits. Bake at 425 degrees untl brown.

MONKEY BREAD

2 pkg dry yeast	1 1/2 tsp salt
1/3 cup shortening	6 cups flour
1/4 cup sugar	butter

Combine yeast and 1 cup luke warm water in bowl and set aside. Cream with mixer shortening, sugar and salt. Add 1 cup boiling water to creamed mixture and stir until shortening melts. Add yeast mixture. Add 3 cups flour and mix with mixer, then add 5 cups flour and mix by hand. Let rise until double. Punch down and roll out. Cut in various shapes and dip in butter. Then place in tube pan. Let rise 30 to 45 minutes. Bake at 350 degrees for 35 minutes.

BUTTERMILK BISCUITS

3 cups flour	1/2 tsp baking soda
6 tbsp shortening	1 1/2 tsp salt
4 tsp baking powder	1 1/2 cups buttermilk

Sift dry ingredients together an work in the shortening with pastry blender, then add buttermilk and stir quickly, until flour is all dampened. Turn onto a floured board and roll out 1" thick. Cut with floured biscuits cutter and place on a greased baking sheet. Le stand 15 minutes then bake at 350 degrees in oven for 12 to 15 minutes.

MEXICAN CORN BREAD

Lightly brown 1 1/2 pounds ground beef, breaking into small pieces as it cooks,drain and set aside.

1 cup yellow cornmeal	2 eggs
4 chopped jalapeno peppers	3/4 tsp salt
1 cup buttermilk	1/2 tsp baking soda
2 tbsp bacon drippings	1 can cream corn
8 oz shredded cheddar cheese	1 onion

Mix together cornmeal,eggs,soda,buttermilk,corn and bacon drippings into well greased skillet, sprinkle one tbsp cornmeal. Add half the cornmeal mixture, sprinkle the ground beef on top. On top of ground beef, sprinkle onion,jalapeno peppers and cheese. Pour the rest of the cornmeal mixture on top of this and bake at 350 degrees for 50 minutes approx.

MEXICAN CORN BREAD

2 tsp baking powder
1 can whole kernel corn
1 lb cracklens, chopped
1 large onion chopped
1 bell pepper chopped
1 3oz jar pimiento chopped
2 cups grated cheddar cheese

3 eggs beaten
8 slices bacon
1 qt buttermilk
1 tsp baking soda
1 tsp red pepper
2 cups corn meal

Mix well and place in refrigerator until ready to cook. Will keep 2 days.
Grease skillet and put into 400 degree preheated oven until hot, then add mix 1
1/2 inches thick. Bake approximately 1 hour or until brown.

Deserts

COMPANY CHEESECAKE

3/4 cup graham cracker crumbs	3 eggs
1/2 cup toasted almonds	2 tbsp butter
1 1/2 lbs cream cheese	2 tsp vanilla
1 cup & 5 tbsp sugar	2 cups sour cream

Butter,cheese and eggs must be at room temperature. Mix crumbs, 2 tbsp of sugar and butter. Press into a large baking pan. Cream the cheese slowly. Beat in one cup of sugar and then add eggs one at a time mixing well. Add one teaspoon vanilla, pour into pan. Bake at 350 degrees for 20 minutes or until set. Time may vary with size of pan. Remove from oven. Increase heat 500 degrees. Mix sour cream and 3 tbsp of sugar and one tsp vanilla or almond flavoring. Spread on cake and bake for 5 minutes. Then chill. This cake is good garnished with a sprinkle of cinnamon or nutmed or toasted almonds.\

RUM CAKE

1/2 cup chopped pecans	1/2 cup water
1 box cake mix(buttered)	1/2 cup oil
1 pkg vanilla instant pudding	4 eggs
1/2 cup light rum	

Sprinkle pecans in bottom of greased and floured pan. Mix remaining ingredients and pour over pecans. Bake at 350 degrees for 60 minutes.

PEANUT BRITTLE

1/2 cup white karo syrup	1/2 cup water
1 cup raw peanuts	1 cup sugar

Mix together and cook on low heat. Boil until peanuts turn a little brown, then add 1 tsp of baking soda and 1 tsp salt. Take off heat. Stir and pour on a buttered plate or pan, after cool break into pieces.

POUND CAKE

1 box powdered sugar
1 cup chopped nuts
1/2 cup canned milk
1/3 cup cocoa

1 tsp vanilla
1 stick butter
1/2 cup coconut

Mix together in pan and boil 1 minute. Stir lightly after taking from heat and add to cake while hot. Cool before cutting.

LEMON PIE

3 egg yolks,unbeaten
1 (9") baked pie shell
3 tbsp cornstarch
1 tbsp grated lemon rind
1/4 cup lemon juice

1 cup sugar
1 cup milk
1/4 cup butter
1 cup sour cream

Combine sugar and cornstarch in saucepan. Add butter,lemon rind,juice and egg yolks. Stir milk. Cook over medium heat, stirring until thick. Cool. Fold in sour cream. Spoon into baked pie sheet. Chill at least 2 hours. Add a garnish of whipped cream before serving.

PECAN CREAM PIE

3/4 cup sugar
3/4 cup chopped pecans
1 cup milk
3 egg yolks

3 tbsp flour
1 tsp vanilla
pinch of salt

Cook custard until, thick, add pecans, whip egg whites. Then add half of egg whites to custard, pour into baked pie shell and cover top with remaining egg whites, then bake in slow-oven untl brown.

CHERRY COBBLER

2 cups cherry pie filliing	2 sticks butter
1 can crushed pineapple	1 cup chopped pecans
1 box yellow or white dry cake mix (2 layer size)	

Use a pan, grease well, spread cans of cherry pie filling on bottom, then spread crushed pineapple with juice over pie filling. Sprinkle dry cake mix over mixture then sprinkle chopped nuts over cake mix. Slice 2 sticks of butter, to cover top of cake mix. Do not stir. Bake at 350 degrees for 45 minutes to 1 hour.

CHOCOLATE PUDDING

1 tsp lemon extract	1 egg
1 stick butter	1 tsp baking soda
1 cup sugar	1 tsp vanilla
2 tbsp of cocoa	1 1/2 cups flour
1 cup buttermilk	

Cream together butter and sugar, add egg, sift together cocoa; flour and soda. Add alternately flour and buttermilk. Ending with flour. Add vanilla and lemon. Bake in a pan. Serve with chocolate sauce.

PEACH COBBLER

1 large can peaches	1 stick butter melted in pan

Drain peaches leaving a little juice in them. Add butter. Mix together.

3/4 cup self-rising flour	3/4 cup reg flour
3/4 cup sugar	

Pour mixture into pan do not stir. Cook in oven at 425 degrees until brown.

FLAKY PIE CRUST

2 cups sifted flour	1/2 tsp salt
6 tbsp ice water	1 cup shortening

Mix flour and salt, cut in shortening, add water using enough to make a workable paste. Roll out pastry and line pan.

GRAHAM CRACKER PIE CRUST

1 pkg graham finely rolled   1/4 cup sugar
1/4 cup butter (softened)

Blend cracker crumbs, sugar and butter, press firmly against bottom and sides
of pie plate. Bake in oven at 375 degrees for 8 minutes then let cool.

VINEGAR PIE

2 cups boiling water   1/3 tsp salt
1 tsp lemon extract   3/4 cup flour
6 tbsp sugar in meringue   1/4 cup apple cider vinegar
3 egg whites for meringue

Mix all ingredients except vinegar, mix with hot water, add vinegar and cook
over boiling water until thick. Pour into baked pie shell and cover with
meringue. Bake until brown.

PECAN PIE

3 eggs slightly beaten   1 cup pecans
1 cup white karo syrup   1/2 tsp salt
1 cup sugar   1 tsp vanilla

Beat eggs, add sugar and blend, add karo and other ingredients then pecans.
Mix well. Bake for 10 minutes at 450 degrees, then turn down to 350 degrees
for approx. 30 minutes.

LEMON PIE

1 cup sugar   12 egg yolks
2 tbsp butter   1 cup milk
2 tbsp flour   3 lemons juiced

Cream butter, sugar and flour, and milk, egg yolks and lemon juice, fold into
stifly beaten egg whites, bake in unbaked pie shell at 350 degrees until slightly
brown on top and center of pie is done.

BANANA PUDDING

1 80z pkg cream cheese	2 1/4 cups milk
1 (3 1/2 oz pkg) vanilla instant pudding and pie filling	
2 cups banana slices	24 vanilla wafers

Combine cream cheese and 1/2 cup milk, mixing until well blended. Add remaining milk and pudding mix, beat for 1 minute. Layer 1/3 of pudding mixture, half of wafers and half of bananas in 1 1/4 qt bowl, repeat layers. Top with remaining pudding, cover and chill.

RICE PUDDING

1/2 cups of rice	1 qt milk
1 tsp grated lemon peel	1/4 tsp nutmeg
1/2 cup seedless raisins	1/2 tsp salt
1/2 cup sugar	

Combine rice, milk, sugar and salt, pour into buttered 1 1/2 qt pan. Bake slow in oven (300 degrees) 1 hour. Stir occasionally. Add lemon peel, nutmeg and raisins, continue baking 1 1/2 to 2 hours.

BUTTERMILK PIE

1/2 cup melted butter	6 eggs
3 1/2 cups sugar	1/2 tsp salt
1 cup buttermilk	1/2 cup flour

Mix ingredients well, pour into unbaked pie shells and bake at 300 degrees until brown. Ground nutmeg sprinkled on pie before baking.

Cookies

COWBOY COOKIES

2 cups sifted flour	1 tsp baking soda
1/2 tsp baking powder	1/4 tsp salt
1 cup shortening	2 eggs
1 cup brown sugar	1 pkg chocolate bits
2 cups rolled oats	1 tsp vanilla
1 cup granulated sugar	

Sift together and set aside. Flour,soda,salt,baking powder. Blend together shortening and sugar. Add eggs and beat until light and fluffy. Add flour and mix well, add rolled oats, vanilla, chocolate bits, dough is crumbly. Drop on greased sheet with tsp, bake 15 minutes at 350 degrees.

GINGER SNAPS

1 cup sugar	1 cup molasses
1 cup butter	1 tbsp vinegar
1 tbsp baking soda	1 egg
1 tbsp ginger	pinch of salt

Flour to form stiff dough, mix molasses, vinegar,sugar,salt,butter and vinegar, and let come to a boil, cool and add soda dissolved in beaten egg. Mix in enough flour to form a stiff dough. Roll and cut into cookies, cook slow in oven.

BUTTER COOKIES

2 sticks butter	2 cups flour
3/4 cup confectioners	1 tsp vanilla

Mix butter, sugar and vanilla. Add flour(stiff dough). Form small balls. Insert pecan half in each ball. Bake at 350 degrees until light brown. Roll in powdered sugar while warm.

MOLASSES COOKIES

1/2 cup shortening
1/2 cup butter
1 cup white sugar
1 cup brown sugar
1 cup dark molasses
1 egg

4 cups flour
2 tsp baking soda
1/2 tsp ginger
1/2 tsp salt
1 tsp lemon extract

Cream first six ingredients. Add flour sifted together with soda, salt and ginger, add lemon extract. Dough should be soft not sticky. Chill 4 hours. Shape into 1 1/2 balls, place 2" apart on greased pan, bake at 350 degrees.

BROWNIE COOKIES

2 bars sweet chocolate
1 tbsp butter
3/4 cup sugar
1/4 cup flour
1/4 tsp cinnamon

3/4 cup pecans
1/4 tsp baking powder
1/2 tsp salt
1/2 tsp vanilla
2 eggs

Melt chocolate and butter over hot water. Cool, beat eggs foamy. Add sugar, 2 tbsp at a time. Beat 5 minutes. Blend in chocolate mixture. Add flour, baking powder, salt and cinnamon. Stir in vanilla and pecans, drop cookies in greased pan. Bake at 350 degrees.

Sauces, Dressings & Gravies

B-B-Q Sauce

1 onion chopped
1 tbsp oil
3 tbsp worcestershire
2 tbsp brown sugar
3 gloves chopped garlic

1 cup ketchup
1/2 tsp mustard
2 tbsp vinegar
1/2 cup water
4 tbsp lemon juice

Saute onion in oil. Add the rest and simmer for 30 minutes.

Cheese Sauce

1 cup grated cheddar cheese
1/2 cup salad dressing

1 tsp onion powder
1 tsp mustard

Heat until melted, stir and serve over vegetables.

Hot Dill Sauce

2 tbsp butter
3 tbsp flour
2/3 cup bouillon

2 tsp lemon juice
2 tbsp fresh dill
salt & pepper

Put butter in sauce pan, smooth in flour, cook slow until it browns a litte. Add bouillon and stir. Add dill(cut fine), then season with lemon juice, salt and pepper. Cook one minute, serve hot.

Horseradish Sauce

3 tbsp grated horseradish
1 tbsp grated onion

1 tbsp lemon juice
1 cup cream sauce

Mix and serve.

TARTER SAUCE

1 tbsp chopped green olives
1 cup mayonnaise
1 tbsp ground onion
1 tbsp ground parsley
Dash paprika

1 tsp horseradish
1 tbsp ground chives
1 tbsp whole capers
1 tbsp chopped pickles

Mix all and serve.

SAUTEED TOMATOES WITH EGG SAUCE

1/2 tbsp grated onion
5 tbsp oil
3 tbsp flour
1 1/2 cup milk
Toast

8 tomatoes
1/2 tsp salt
1/3 tsp pepper
3 hard cooked eggs

Cut the washed stemmed tomatoes in halves and dip in seasoned flour. Saute in 4 tbsp oil until tender, turning once. Arrange on buttered toast. Then put 3 tbsp oil in frying pan, and onion, flour and stir until smooth. Then add milk, salt and pepper and stir until blended and thickened. Pour over the tomatoes and garnish with eggs. Cut in eighths.

SAVORY SALAD DRESSING

1 tbsp dry mustard
1/2 tbsp worcestershire sauce
1 1/3 cups ketchup
1/2 cup vinegar
1 cup salad oil

2 tsp sugar
1/2 tsp salt
1/8 tsp celery salt
dash cayenne pepper

Mix all ingredients until thoroughly combines.

HORSERADISH SAUCE

3 tbsp horseradish
1/2 cup whipped cream

1/4 tsp salt

Fold horseradish and salt in the whipped cream.

Russian Dressing

12 tbsp mayonnaise
3 tbsp pimientos
12 sprigs minced chives
1 tbsp tarragon vinegar

6 tbsp chili sauce
1 tsp chopped capers
3 tbsp whipped cream

Mix in order given, chill well and serve.

Thousand Island Dressing

2 hard cooked eggs, chopped
2 tbsp finely chopped pimientos
2 tbsp minced chives
1/2 cup heavy cream

1/2 cup mayonnaise
2 tbsp tomato catsup
2 tbsp chili sauce

Mix in order given and chill.

Curry Sauce

2 tbsp butter
1/2 tbsp lemon juice
1 tbsp curry powder

2 tbsp flour
1 cup milk
1 chopped onion

Melt butter in the top of double broiler, add the onion, and cook about 2 minutes, but do not brown, add the curry and flour mixed together. Stir until smooth. Stir in the milk, cook until thickened, stirring constantly. Add lemon juice. Place over boiling water in lower part of double broiler and let it cook 5 minutes longer.

Gravy

Make gravy in the pan in which meat or poultry was roasted. If there is too much oil for the gravy, pour off some, place pan over the heat, add flour equal in amount to the oil. Blend well, and stir until golden brown. Add 3/8 cup cold water or milk for each tbsp of flour. Boil until perfectly smooth, stirring constantly. Season with salt and pepper.

Red Eye Gravy

Leave the brown drippings from frying ham in the skillet, put equal amount of hot water. Scrape skillet until all crumbs are loose. Ready to serve.

White Sauce (for potatoes)

2 tbsp butter   2 tbsp flour
1/8 tsp salt   1 cup milk
pepper

Melt butter and stir in pepper,salt and flour until smooth. Add milk. Cook slowly until it boils and thickens.

Giblet and Mushroom Gravy

Cook chicken or turkey giblets until tender, drain and cut in small pieces,saving liquor. Saute sliced mushrooms caps from 1 lb of mushrooms until golden brown in the left in the roasting pan, as in gravy, add an equal amount of flour, blend and add liquid as in gravy, using giblet lliquor part of it. Add the chopped giblets. Cook mushrooms stems in 2 cups water for 20 minutes. Strain and use liquor in gravy.

B-B-Q Sauce

1/2 cup vinegar   1/2 cup catsup
1 tbsp worcestershire sauce   1 tbsp salt
1/2 tsp hot pepper sauce   1 onion diced
1/2 tsp chili powder   dash of sage
2 gloves garlic diced

Combine all ingredients stir and simmer for 15 minutes.

Currant Mint Sauce

1 glass currant jelly   2 tbsp minced mint
2 tbsp orange rind shavings   leaves

Break up the jelly, but do not beat it. Add the mint leaves and orange rind.

BASTING SAUCE

1/2 cup catsup	2 tbsp vinegar
1 tbsp prepared mustard	2 tbsp honey
dash of hot pepper sauce	2 tsp kitchen
bouquet	

Combine all, mix. Use immediately or store in refrigerator.

CHICKEN DRESSING

6 cups corn meal	1 stick butter
1 stalk celery,chopped fine	3 cups flour
2 large onions,chopped fine	8 eggs
1 cup buttermilk	

Mix above ingredients, add baked bread. Crumble bread, add salt,pepper and poultry seasoning. Add chicken broth until desired.

MAYONNAISE

1 egg	2 tsp mustard
3/4 cup oil	1 cup water
1/4 cup vinegar	4 tbsp cornstarch
1 tsp salt	1/4 tsp paprika
1 1/2 tbsp sugar	

Put egg, oil, vinegar and seasonings in large mixing bowl. Cook water and cornstarch until thick and clear. Mix all and heat until smooth and thick. Chill before using.

Drinks

Eggnog

1 qt ice cream	1 cup liquor
1 cup whipping cream	1 1/2 cup coffee

Whip cream. Blend all and serve.

Frosted White Punch

2 cans pineapple juice(large)	1 bottle ale
1 pt pineapple sherbet	

Mix all and add crushed ice.

Red Hot Cider

1 qt apple cider	1/2 cups red hots

Heat apple cider and red hots until melted. Serve hot

Wassail

2 qts apple juice	2/3 cup lemon juice
1 whole stick cinnamon	1 can orange juice(18 oz)
1 tsp whole cloves	1 cup sugar
1 can pineapple juice(46 oz)	

Simmer apple juice, cinnamon and cloves for 5 to 10 minutes. Add other ingredients and heat. Strain and serve hot

Light Sparkle

Use equal amounts of ice cold 7-up and apple cider.

Scarlet Duck

1 qt cranberry juice   1 4/5ths bottle cold duck
1 28 oz bottle 7-up

Have all ingredients cold. Add to punch bowl in the order given. Do not stir.

Rum Eggnog

1 jigger sherbert   1/4 cup cream
1 tbsp simple syrup   1/2 cup milk
1 tbsp cognac   nutmeg
1 egg

Blend.

Green Mist

1 qt lime sherbert   3 – 28 oz bottles 7-up
1 qt pineapple sherbert   3 – 28 oz bottles squirt

Soften and blend the two sherberts, then gently add 7-up and squirt.

Strawberry Punch

1 large can crushed pineapple   1 pt strawberries
1 pkg strawberry kool-aid   2 cups boiling water
1 small bottle lemon juice   3 cups sugar
3 qts water

Mix boiling water and sugar until sugar dissolves. Then refrigerate until cold. Add remaining ingredients and serve.

Spiced Tea

9 oz orange tang   1/2 cup sugar
1/3 cup instant tea   1 tsp cinnamon
1/4 tsp cloves crushed

Mix cranberry, pineapple and sugar. Add ginger ale at serving.

Quantities to serve 100 people

Coffee	3 lbs
Loaf sugar	3 lbs
Cream	3 quarts
Whipping cream	4 pints
Milk	6 gallons
Fruit cocktail	2 1/2 gallons
Fruit juice	4 no. 10 cans(26 lbs)
Tomato juice	4 no. 10 cans(26 lbs)
Soup	5 gallons
Oysters	18 quarts
Weiners	25 lbs
Meat loaf	24 lbs
Ham	40 lbs
Beef	40 lbs
Roast beef	40 lbs
Hamburger	30-36 lbs
Chicken for chicken pie	40 lbs
Potatoes	35 lbs
Scalloped potatoes	5 gallons
Vegetables	4 no. 10 cans(26 lbs)
Baken beans	5 gallons
Beets	30 lbs
Cauliflower	18 lbs
Cabbage for slaw	20 lbs
Carrots	33 lbs
Bread	10 loaves
Rolls	200
Butter	3 lbs
Potato salad	12 quarts
Fruit salad	20 quarts
Vegetable salad	20 quarts
Lettuce	20 heads
Salad dressing	3 quarts
Pies	18
Cakes	8
Ice cream	4 gallons
Cheese	3 lbs
Olives	1 1/2 lbs
Pickles	2 quarts
Nuts	3 lbs sorted

Notes: